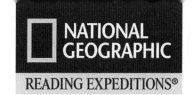

W9-AYA-143

EYEWITNESS

# The Eruption of Mount St. Helens

By Rebecca L. Johnson
Illustrated by Rick Wheeler

**Picture Credits**
4, 7, 13, 14, 19, 20, 23, 24, 27, 39, 41, 44, 46, 50, 55, 56, 62 (icon art) Rick Wheeler; 4 Tom and Pat Leeson; 5 (top to bottom) © David Muench/Corbis; (map) Mapping Specialists, Ltd.; 62 © Gary Braasch/Corbis; 63 © Roger Ressmeyer/Corbis; 64 (diagram) Precision Graphics; 65 © Steve Raymer/National Geographic Society; 66 (top to bottom) © Steve Raymer/National Geographic Society, © Darrell Gulin/Corbis; 68 (background) © T. Kitchin/V. Hurst/Photo Researchers; (bottom left) © G. Brad Lewis/The Stone Collection/Getty Images; (bottom right) © Carsten Peter/National Geographic Image Collection.

Produced through the worldwide resources of the National Geographic Society, John M. Fahey, Jr., President and Chief Executive Officer; Gilbert M. Grosvenor, Chairman of the Board; Nina D. Hoffman, Executive Vice President and President, Books and Education Publishing Group.

**Prepared by National Geographic School Publishing**
Ericka Markman, Senior Vice President and President, Children's Books and Education Publishing Group; Steve Mico, Senior Vice President, Publisher, Editorial Director; Francis Downey, Executive Editor; Richard Easby, Editorial Manager; Bea Jackson, Director of Design; Cindy Olson, Art Director; Margaret Sidlosky, Director of Illustrations; Matt Wascavage, Manager of Publishing Services; Lisa Pergolizzi, Sean Philpotts, Production Managers, Ted Tucker, Production Specialist.

**Manufacturing and Quality Control**
Christopher A. Liedel, Chief Financial Officer; Phillip L. Schlosser, Director; Clifton M. Brown, Manager.

**Editors**
Barbara Seeber, Mary Anne Wengel

**Book Development**
Morrison BookWorks LLC

**Book Design**
Steven Curtis Design

**Art Direction**
Dan Banks, Project Design Company

Published by the National Geographic Society
1145 17th Street, N.W.
Washington, D.C. 20036-4688

ISBN: 0-7922-5862-2

2012 2013 2014 2015
 2 3 4 5 6 7 8 9 10 11 12 13 14 15

# CONTENTS

The Setting –
Before the Eruption............ 4

Chapter 1 ................... 7
*In the Mountain's Shadow*

Chapter 2 ................... 14
*The Farm in the Valley*

Chapter 3 ................... 20
*A Shudder in the Earth*

Chapter 4 ................... 27
*The Mountain Comes to Life*

Chapter 5 ................... 41
*More Changes on the Mountain*

Chapter 6 ................... 46
*Eruption!*

Chapter 7 ................... 56
*Aftermath*

The Facts Behind the Story ... 62

Read, Research, and Write..... 67

Extend Your Reading.......... 68

# Mount St. Helens

MOUNT ST. HELENS rises thousands of feet above the hills and valleys of Washington State. The mountain is part of the Cascade Mountain range.

Mount St. Helens is covered in trails. People come from all over the country to hike, camp and fish on and near Mount St. Helens. The dense forests on the mountain supply the logging industry. Many local people work as loggers.

Those who live in the area know that this enormous mountain is a volcano. Most people are not worried, though, because it hasn't erupted for nearly 130 years.

▲ People enjoy hiking, camping and fishing on and near Mount St. Helens.

▲ Mount St. Helens before 1980

## Mount St. Helens and Surrounding Area – Before the Eruption

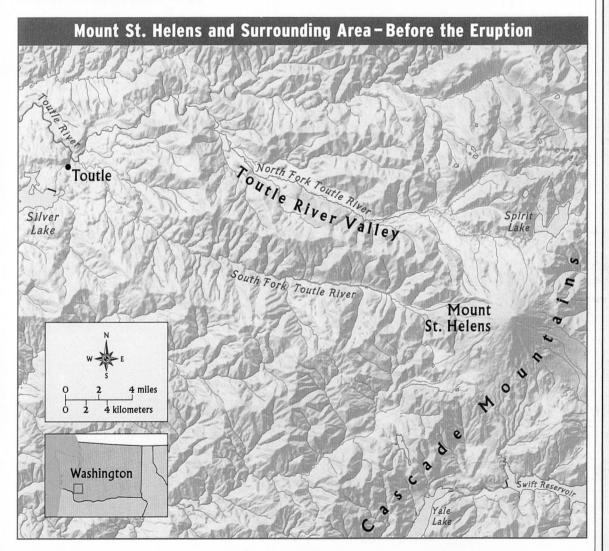

Toutle River

Toutle

Silver Lake

North Fork Toutle River

Toutle River Valley

Spirit Lake

South Fork Toutle River

Mount St. Helens

Cascade Mountains

N
W — E
S

0   2   4 miles
0   2   4 kilometers

Washington

Swift Reservoir

Yale Lake

# CHAPTER 1

# In the Mountain's Shadow

 **LIKE A MIRROR,** the surface of Spirit Lake held a perfect image of Mount St. Helens. Helen Crenshaw studied the volcano's reflection in the still water. Then she raised her eyes to look at the real thing. It was so beautiful. She never got tired of looking at it. A nearly perfect cone, Mount St. Helens towered over the landscape. Its snowcapped peak gleamed pure white against the blue sky.

Helen turned at the sound of a fishing line whipping through the air. The lure landed lightly on the water. It made tiny ripples that broke up the mountain's reflection. A split second later, a big trout struck the lure. The line went tight. Tom Crenshaw let out a soft cry and grinned. Helen watched her father reel in the fish. He was the best fisherman in the Toutle River Valley.

Wind sighed through the tall evergreen trees that surrounded the lake. Helen stood up, adjusting her cap over her long brown hair. She was tall for her age. It was a trait she'd inherited from her father. Tom was six feet four inches tall. Helen was nearly a head taller than most of the kids in her fifth grade class. She was even taller than some of the sixth graders.

"I'm going for a walk, Dad," Helen called out. Her father nodded, not bothering to look away from the fish he'd landed. "OK. But keep it short, Helen," he said. "And find Chad. We need to head home soon."

Helen stepped lightly up the bank and slipped into the trees. Their massive trunks were straight and tall. Their roots hugged ground that was soft and damp. Winter had finally lost its grip on the Cascade Mountains here in southwestern Washington. It was mid-March. Spring flowers were blooming. Helen spotted some wild strawberry plants. It wouldn't be long before there would be all kinds of ripe and juicy berries to pick—raspberries, strawberries, blackberries. Helen liked wild salmonberries best. Her mother had loved them too.

Some days Helen felt like she'd lost her mother a long time ago. But it had happened just last year, in 1979. Sometime in March, Laura Crenshaw started complaining about feeling unusually tired. Then the pain had come. "I'm sure it's nothing," she'd told Helen. "The doctors will give me a shot or a pill and I'll be fine." But it wasn't "nothing." It was cancer, a kind that couldn't be cured.

In the weeks that followed, Helen's mother grew more and more ill. There was nothing the doctors could do. And then, on a rainy day last June, Laura Crenshaw had died. Helen had felt like the bottom dropped out of her world.

Helen tried to ignore the sudden tightness in her throat. "Think about something else," she said to herself. She tipped back her head and stared up at the treetops. She could see the peak of Mount St. Helens through them. Seeing the mountain always made Helen feel better. It was familiar and constant, like an old friend. Helen knew every detail of the north slope—how the trees hugged the mountainside and how the glaciers at the top curved down to meet them.

Helen knew, as everyone in the valley did, that Mount St. Helens was a volcano. But in all the years that Helen had lived in its shadow, the mountain had only given out an occasional puff of steam and smoke.

Birds called from all around as Helen moved deeper into the trees. From up ahead came the soft gurgling of a stream. Melted snow from Mount St. Helens fed Spirit Lake. Every winter the glaciers grew thick with a new layer of snow and ice. And every spring, some of that winter snow melted in the warm sun. The water fed the streams that wound through the forest and eventually joined the rivers that ran through the valley.

Helen reached the stream. It was wider than she remembered it being last fall. The spring meltwater had swelled it. Helen guessed her brother was somewhere on the other side. No doubt he was climbing trees or clambering over boulders. There were few things Chad liked to do more than explore the forest, except for climbing the volcano's steep slopes. He'd climbed to the crater several times. It was something Helen hoped to do this summer. Maybe the next time he went, she'd get to go along. *Yeah, right,* Helen said to herself, knowing how her brother would complain if anyone suggested he take his little sister with him!

Helen walked along the edge of the stream. She looked for a place to cross. Finally she spotted a fallen tree trunk. It stretched across to the other bank. Helen stepped up onto the trunk. It was covered with slippery moss. Her sneakers slid on the bark.

"You can do this," Helen muttered to herself. But from deep inside her head came a tiny voice that said, "Are you sure?"

Helen frowned and clenched her fists. This was silly. She used to balance on fallen logs all the time. Helen took another step. Now she was out over the water. She teetered to one side. What was wrong with her? Over the last few months, she'd felt this way often. It was as if her confidence suddenly deserted her.

*It's just ten steps across a log,* Helen thought. *Why does it seem so hard?* Now her heart was pounding. "Just walk across," Helen whispered fiercely to herself. But as she started to take the next step, she could feel her faith in herself slipping away. With it went her balance. Helen's feet slid out from underneath her. She tumbled off the log and fell into the stream.

The water was only knee-deep. But it was freezing cold! Helen gasped as she stood up. Her shirt and jeans were soaked. Shivering, she slogged through the stream and climbed up the bank.

"Way to go, sis!" Helen whirled toward the sound of her brother's voice. Chad Crenshaw was standing on top of a big boulder a few yards away. He grinned down at his little sister. "You've won the klutz-of-the-day award!"

Helen glared up at him. "I just lost my balance," she snapped.

Chad jumped down from the boulder. He strode over to where Helen stood dripping. For sixteen, he was tall for his age, just like his sister. "Well," he said with a smirk, "I suggest you try to find it again before you go crossing any more streams."

"Dad sent me to find you," Helen said, changing the subject. "It's time to go home."

Chad frowned. He'd planned to climb up onto the mountain. It was Sunday. Why did they have to hurry back?

Helen read the look on his face. "He said we had to go. I don't know why."

Chad turned and walked off toward the lake, muttering under his breath. Helen followed, hoping her clothes would dry before they got there.

Tom was waiting for his children by the lakeshore. The fish was already on ice. He'd packed up the car and was ready to go. "What happened to you?" Tom asked his daughter when Helen was close enough for him to see her damp clothes.

"It's nothing!" Helen exclaimed. "I just slipped and fell in a stream."

Out of the corner of her eye, Helen caught the smirk on her brother's face. Angrily, she whirled to face him. But before either of his children could say another word, Tom stepped quickly between them.

"No fighting, you two," he said firmly. "It's Sunday, OK? Just give it a rest."

Helen's eyes flashed. Then she spun on her heel and hurried off toward the car. Tom turned to his son with an exasperated look. "What is it with you two these days, Chad?" Tom asked. "Can't you at least try to get along?" Chad just shrugged his shoulders and headed for the car.

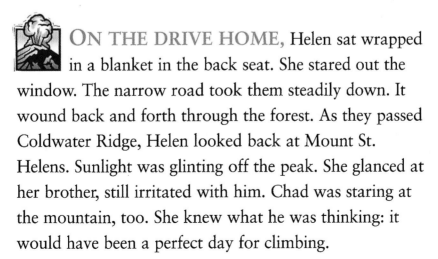 ON THE DRIVE HOME, Helen sat wrapped in a blanket in the back seat. She stared out the window. The narrow road took them steadily down. It wound back and forth through the forest. As they passed Coldwater Ridge, Helen looked back at Mount St. Helens. Sunlight was glinting off the peak. She glanced at her brother, still irritated with him. Chad was staring at the mountain, too. She knew what he was thinking: it would have been a perfect day for climbing.

# CHAPTER 2

# The Farm in the Valley

 AFTER A FEW MORE BENDS in the road, Helen looked out at the green wonder of the Toutle River Valley. Her eyes followed the gentle curves of the north fork of the Toutle River. It began at Spirit Lake and flowed gently past stands of tall trees and patches of rolling meadow. Helen caught sight of red-brown bodies and big antlers. A herd of elk was drinking at the river's edge.

Steep hills rose up on either side of the river valley. The hillsides were thick with evergreen trees that grew straight and tall and very close together. The forest covered the hillsides and crept halfway up the slopes of Mount St. Helens.

From the back seat, Helen turned to watch her father drive. He hadn't said a word since they'd left the lake. It was strange for him to be so quiet. He seemed lost in thought as he sat behind the steering wheel, following the narrow dirt road almost mechanically. Helen's father knew these roads better than most people in the valley. As a logger, he spent most of his days in the forests that covered the hillsides. The logging company he worked for owned thousands of acres of land around Mount St. Helens. Logging allowed her father to spend most of his time outdoors. Like Helen, he loved being outside.

The landscape leveled out as they reached the river valley. Small farms hugged the banks of the river. Off in the distance, Helen could see the south fork of the Toutle River winding its way north. They were almost home. The Crenshaw place was very close to where the two forks of the river came together.

At the red mailbox lettered with "Crenshaw," Tom turned off the highway and into the drive. Tires crunched on the gravel. A few chickens hurried to get out of the way.

"There's Grandma Rae!" Helen cried. After the car had rolled to a stop, she flung open the door. She bounded out toward a small, slim woman with short gray hair.

Helen threw her arms around her grandmother. Rae Everest hugged her granddaughter hard. Then she held her at arms' length and looked closely at Helen's clothes.

"You're as damp as my basement on a rainy day, child," Rae said. "What happened?"

"Nothing happened, Grandma," Helen sighed, taking a step backward. All she wanted to do was forget about her slip into the stream. As her father and Chad walked up, Helen turned and ran across the front yard. She trotted up the steps and into the house.

"Hello, Rae," Tom said, as Chad got a hug from his grandmother. "What brings you out here on this lovely Sunday morning?"

"I baked you a pie," Rae replied. "I left it in the kitchen. I didn't know you'd be down from the mountain so soon."

"Dad made us come back early," Chad said, with an edge to his voice. But he smiled as he said, "Where's that pie? I'm starving!"

Tom and Rae followed Chad into the house. It was an old house, with windows that looked out on the river and up the valley. A small apple orchard lay between the house and the river. To one side stretched a pasture where a dozen cows grazed. Angling off on the other side was a freshly plowed field, waiting to be planted.

Helen came into the kitchen wearing dry clothes. Her grandmother sensed she didn't want to talk about what had happened. The four of them sat around the old oak table and devoured half the pie.

"OK, you two," said Tom, when they'd finished. "There are chores to be done. And Helen, I seem to remember that you've got some homework to finish."

As soon as the children were out of the house, Rae set down her coffee cup and gave Tom a searching look. "What happened to Helen up at the lake?" she asked.

"She says she lost her balance crossing a stream," Tom replied.

"That girl is as graceful as a gazelle," Rae said. "It doesn't sound like her at all."

"Well, I wouldn't give it much thought myself, except it's not the first time something like this has happened," Tom responded. He lowered his voice a little. "Helen hasn't been herself lately. She doesn't seem to trust herself anymore. It's like she's afraid to make decisions."

"What else has happened?" Rae asked.

Tom leaned forward in his chair. "Last week she was out riding her horse, Jake. She's jumped that low fence into the pasture dozens of times. I was watching her. At the last second, she seemed to falter. Like she wasn't sure she could do it. Jake pulled up short and she nearly fell off. I think the horse sensed her doubt." He said.

Rae was quiet for a moment. "You know, Tom," she began. "People react differently to losing someone they love. It wouldn't surprise me if Helen's lack of confidence is somehow linked to that."

"I know," Tom replied. He was silent for a long time. "Everywhere I look there's something to remind me of Laura. It's so hard not having her here. I'm beginning to wonder if leaving wouldn't be the best thing for Helen and Chad . . . and me. Maybe a change would do us all a lot of good."

 HELEN HAD FINISHED feeding the chickens and giving Jake some oats. As she walked across the yard, she could see Chad out in the pasture, checking the cattle. Helen slipped quietly into the house and started down the hallway to her room. She didn't mean to eavesdrop. But she couldn't help overhearing what her father was saying.

"I've been looking into a forest service job in Montana, Rae," Tom said heavily. "It would be a new start. There are just too many memories here. It just hurts too much."

Helen didn't wait to hear her grandmother's reply. She ran down the hallway to her room. She flung herself on her bed and stared out the window. She could see the river from her room.

# CHAPTER 3

# A Shudder in the Earth

 HELEN SAID LITTLE at breakfast the next morning. She packed her lunch and was soon pedaling down the road. Her school was in Toutle, a small town about a mile west of the farm. The ride into town was mostly downhill. Helen passed the gas station and turned up Main Street. A few minutes later she parked her bike in front of the school. The bell rang as she hurried inside.

The day didn't start well. Helen's teacher surprised her class with a spelling test. Three of the ten words Mrs. Davis read out didn't look quite right when Helen wrote them down. That nagging question returned: "Are you sure?" So she changed all three. Even before Mrs. Davis read out the correct spellings, Helen knew her spellings were wrong. She got a C on the test. *Why did I doubt myself?* Helen wondered. Discouraged, she got out her science book. Just flipping through the pages made Helen feel a little better. She loved science.

Helen's class had been studying volcanoes for about two weeks. Each student had to choose a volcano and write a report about it. Then they were to give an oral report to the class. Quite a few kids chose to research Mount Etna in Sicily. Several more picked Kilauea in Hawaii. Only Helen had chosen Mount St. Helens.

"Mount St. Helens?" Ricky Hofer had sneered when Helen announced her choice. "Who'd want to report on such a boring volcano? It's been dead for more than a hundred years."

"Just because a volcano doesn't erupt regularly doesn't mean it's dead," Helen had replied.

"You just picked Mount St. Helens because you were named after it!" Ricky had shot back.

"I was not!" Helen had retorted hotly. "I was named after my great-grandmother!"

"Careful, Ricky," another boy had chimed in. "If you make her angry enough, Mount St. Helens might blow her top!"

Today was March 17, the day Helen was scheduled to give her volcano report to the class. Ricky started to snicker as soon as Helen got up in front of the class. But she shot him a look that silenced him. "My report is on Mount St. Helens," Helen began. "The mountain has been quiet for so long that it's easy to forget St. Helens is a volcano."

Helen went on to tell her classmates how Mount St. Helens is located along the border where two **tectonic plates** that make up Earth's crust come together. On a poster she'd made, Helen pointed out how the smaller plate slides under the much larger North American Plate. As the smaller plate slides down, she explained, great pressure causes rock to melt. This melted rock, or **magma,** sometimes pushes up to the surface.

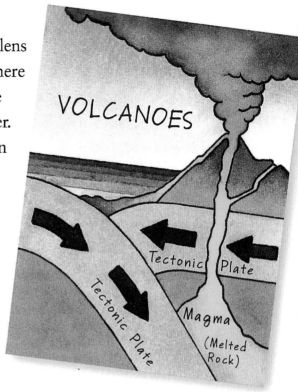

"You all know by now that when **magma** erupts it's called **lava**," Helen continued. "And lava cools to form volcanic rock. Over thousands of years, repeated eruptions formed the towering peak of Mount St. Helens. They also formed other volcanic peaks in the Cascade Mountains."

Helen held up a copy of an old sketch of the mountain. "Long before the explorer, Vancouver, arrived," Helen

**tectonic plate** – a large slab of Earth's outer layer, or crust
**magma** – melted rock beneath Earth's crust
**lava** – magma that has erupted onto Earth's surface

continued, "Mount St. Helens filled native peoples with a mix of fear and awe. All the tribes in the area around Mount St. Helens knew that when the mountain erupted, it meant danger, even death, for everything living near it."

"The last time Mount St. Helens was active," Helen said, "was in the 1850s. It's been pretty quiet ever since."

"Like I said, it's a boring volcano," muttered Rick, just loud enough for most of the class to hear.

"Scientists know that Mount St. Helens could erupt again," Helen replied, looking straight at Ricky. "They just don't know when."

 IT HAD BEEN A LONG DAY at school. Helen was relieved when the bell rang. She grabbed her books, hopped on her bike, and rode a few blocks to the little coffee shop at the edge of town that her grandmother owned and ran. The sign over the front window read "Rae's Café."

The smell of fresh-baked cookies greeted Helen as she entered the café. Rae was behind the counter, making a big pot of coffee. Helen glanced around. She heaved a soft sigh of relief. The café was empty. Good. She'd been waiting to talk to her grandmother all day.

"You're in luck—I just made a batch of oatmeal cookies," Rae said. She set a plateful of them on the counter. Helen hopped up onto one of the stools. She took a cookie, but couldn't bring herself to take a bite. Rae poured her granddaughter a glass of milk. From the look on Helen's face, she knew something was wrong. She set the milk down and waited.

The big clock above the coffee pot ticked loudly. Finally Helen looked up at her grandmother and said, "Yesterday I heard you and Dad talking. He said something about moving to Montana and making a fresh start." Helen shook her head. "Grandma, I don't want to leave."

Rae came around from behind the counter. She sat down on a stool beside Helen. "I know that, honey," she said quietly. "I'm not quite sure what your Dad has in mind. I do know that he loves you and wants what's best for you and your brother. But I also know that change is hard. And it usually comes when we least expect it."

Helen left the café feeling much better. Talking had helped. She'd promised her grandmother that she'd stop by after school on Thursday.

THE NEXT FEW DAYS passed quickly. When the bell rang Thursday afternoon, Helen was the first one out the door. Minutes later she was at the café.

Rae was busy making a berry cobbler. "Helen, can you keep an eye on things up front for a bit?" she asked. "I've got to get this cobbler in the oven."

Helen went behind the counter. She made Harry
Edwards a sandwich and a malt for his little boy. Then
she walked around the café, refilling customers' coffee cups.

All of a sudden, a shudder passed through the ground.
The room seemed to quiver around Helen. Cups clattered
in their saucers.

"It's an earthquake!" Harry Edwards cried. The
shaking got worse. There was a strange rumbling sound
that grew louder and louder. Helen grabbed the edge of a
table to steady herself. Some plates fell off the counter. Rae

came running out from the kitchen, her eyes wide. Plaster dust drifted past Helen's face. She looked up to see the light fixtures above her head swinging wildly back and forth. If they fall, Helen thought, they'll fall right on me!

But before Helen could move out of the way, the shaking stopped as quickly as it had started. For a moment, everything was eerily silent. Then the little Edwards boy started to cry. Rae strode over to Helen and took the coffee pot from her hand. It wasn't until then that Helen noticed she was shaking.

"That was a good one," Rae said quietly, glancing around the café. "But not a lot of damage done." She went over to pick up the broken pieces of china off the floor.

Helen brushed the dust from her shirt and went to get a broom. She'd felt earthquakes before. She knew from her research on volcanoes that earthquakes weren't uncommon in places where two tectonic plates came together, like they did along the Cascades. But Helen didn't remember ever feeling the earth shake so hard before.

# CHAPTER 4

# The Mountain Comes to Life

 THERE WAS NOTHING on the news about the earthquake that evening. Helen checked the paper the next day. There was no mention of an earthquake near Mount St. Helens on March 20. Maybe it hadn't been as strong as Helen had thought. Most everyone Helen talked to about Thursday's quake dismissed it as "no big deal."

Over the weekend, however, Helen thought she felt the ground shudder slightly several different times. She asked Chad and her father about it while they were all sitting on the porch Sunday afternoon.

"Well, I haven't felt anything," said Chad, leaning against one of the porch steps. "I think you're imagining things, sis."

"Well, not so fast, Chad," said Tom, thoughtfully. "Now that I think of it, I can't say I've felt anything either. But some people are more sensitive than others to these sorts of things. It's possible Helen is just feeling

**aftershocks.** They're like little earthquakes that come after a larger one."

Tom's suggestion made Helen feel a little bit better. All the rest of the day she stayed alert for more aftershocks. But she didn't feel anything unusual in the ground beneath her feet. When she climbed into bed, she lay perfectly still, thinking it might help. But the bed and the room around her seemed as solid as a rock.

Helen was disappointed. Thursday's earthquake had been a little scary. But mostly it was exciting. As she lay in bed, she imagined what might be going on deep underground, where enormously huge plates pressed against each other, and hot magma lay trapped beneath the surface.

When Helen pedaled her bike into Toutle Monday morning for school, she noticed several cars she'd never seen before. Some had government license plates and "USGS" lettered on the driver's door. Maybe this has to do with the earthquake, Helen thought excitedly. Maybe after school she could find out.

When Helen arrived at her grandmother's café, she noticed right away how busy it was. "Hi, Grandma," Helen called out. Rae smiled as Helen slipped behind the counter. Helen nodded toward a table of men she didn't

---

**aftershock** – a small earthquake, usually one of several, that follows a larger one

recognize. They were talking earnestly among themselves. They looked excited. "What's going on?" Helen asked her grandmother softly. "Who are they?"

"Scientists," Rae replied. "I gather some are from the University up in Seattle. One is from the U.S. Geological Survey. Obviously, somebody noticed that earthquake last week. From what I've been able to figure out it seems something important is happening with our volcano."

Helen's heart seemed to skip a beat. Was Mount St. Helens becoming active again? Was it going to erupt? It seemed hard to believe. Yet from all the research Helen had done, she knew almost anything was possible with volcanoes. They were hard to study. Scientists could rarely tell just what a volcano was going to do next. Predicting exactly when a volcano was going to erupt was almost impossible.

Helen helped her grandmother serve food and drinks. Whenever it looked like the scientists needed more coffee, Helen hurried over with the pot. She took her time pouring it, though. Without being rude, she tried to learn as much as she could from the scientists' conversation.

A scientist with a bushy beard was talking about **seismometers.** He said that there were several of the instruments set up on Mount St. Helens. Last Thursday, when the earthquake rattled dishes in Rae's Café, a researcher at the University of Washington in Seattle was monitoring information from seismometers on Mount St. Helens. He noticed the earthquake, and he discovered that it originated directly under the mountain.

"It's the strongest earthquake that's been recorded in the Cascades since the seismometers were installed," the bearded scientist said. "A 4.0 on the **Richter scale.**"

"What does that mean?" Helen blurted out the question without thinking. "Oh, uh . . . sorry . . . I didn't mean to be nosy."

"That's OK," said the bearded scientist with a smile. "The Richter scale is a way to measure earthquakes. Using the scale, earthquakes are given a number, depending on how strong they are. Each number going

**seismometer** – an instrument used to record movements in Earth's crust and show when and where earthquakes are taking place

**Richter scale** – a scientific measure of the strength of an earthquake

up the scale is ten times more powerful than the previous one. For example, a quake that measures 2.0 is 10 times more powerful than one that measures 1.0. Get it?"

Helen nodded. "So an earthquake that measures 3.0 on the scale is ten times stronger than a 2.0 quake, and a hundred times stronger than a 1.0 quake," she replied.

"Very good!" exclaimed the scientist. "The earthquake you folks might have felt here in Toutle last Thursday measured a 4.0. That's a good-size quake. Not big, but strong enough to get our attention. Ever since, we've been detecting lots of aftershocks. Most of them are really small. But they've been occurring pretty often over the past few days."

"Really?" Helen was secretly pleased. What she'd felt hadn't been her imagination. The ground had been shaking off and on over the weekend!

"What's especially interesting to us," the scientist continued, "is that the number of aftershocks is increasing. Most are so minor that only our seismometers can detect them. But believe it or not, they're coming at a rate of more than one per minute right now!"

"What does that mean?" Helen asked.

"Well, it could mean that something's going on under Mount St. Helens. That it's becoming more active," he replied. He paused and looked at Helen kindly. "But don't worry. The activity could also stop as quickly as it started.

We don't really know. That's why we're here—to see if we can figure out what's happening under your mountain."

After the scientists left, Helen sat down at the counter. It was exciting listening to them talk. But it was a little scary, too. Helen tried to imagine what an earthquake that was a 5.0 or even an 8.0 on the Richter scale might feel like. What would happen to the mountain if a bigger earthquake rumbled beneath it? Would it erupt? And if that happened, what would happen to the valley and everything in and around it?

Rae had been watching Helen since the scientists left. She came around the counter and sat down beside her.

"Helen," she said rather sternly, "don't you worry about all this talk about earthquakes and Richter scales and such. Five years ago Mount Baker started to rumble a bit. Scientists issued a warning that it might erupt. It never did, but they scared a lot of people."

Helen nodded. She'd heard people scoff at the idea of Mount St. Helens erupting all her life. But still, what had happened over the last few days was interesting. That evening, sitting at the dinner table with her father and Chad, Helen told them what the scientists had said. Like Rae, Tom was skeptical.

"I've lived here all my life, Helen," he said, "and that mountain's been perfectly harmless. I'm not ready to change my opinion about that."

"Well, I think an eruption would be cool," said Chad. "It would be such an amazing thing to see a mountain blow its top off!"

Helen wasn't as sure as her father that Mount St. Helens was harmless. The scientists had seemed pretty intense. That night she had trouble getting to sleep. The idea of leaving the valley had been bad enough. Now it seemed she had to worry about the mountain changing, too.

The next day when Tom came home from work, he reported that the Forest Service had sealed off the mountain above the timberline. "They evacuated the ranger station at Pine Creek, too," he added.

"You mean we can't go up on the mountain?" Chad asked in disbelief. "But Dave Ford and I were planning to climb to the crater this weekend, if the weather was OK."

"Well, Chad," Tom responded, "I guess you and Dave are out of luck until this whole fuss blows over. And it will," he added, looking at Helen.

But it didn't blow over. On Thursday, March 27, Helen was eating lunch at school. Suddenly, a loud rumble was heard in the distance. It came from the direction of Mount St. Helens.

Helen learned what had happened a few hours later. The news spread through school like wildfire. There had been an explosion near the top of the volcano. Steam and

black ash were shooting thousands of feet up into the air from a new crater that had opened up near the mountain's top. Great cracks ran out from the edge of the crater in several places. The mountain's north slope had changed, too. Now it sagged ever so slightly, as if something beneath the surface had caved in.

Something was definitely going on inside Mount St. Helens. But would it really erupt and spout lava? Or would it simply calm down and go back to being the peaceful mountain it had been for so many years? That night on television, Helen watched David Johnston, one of the scientists studying the volcano, being interviewed about the volcano. He said that being close to Mount St. Helens was like standing next to a keg of dynamite with a fuse that was lit. Except no one knew how long the fuse was.

Over the next few days, Toutle and other nearby towns, such

as Castle Rock, Kelso, and Longview, were flooded with people. Some were scientists—mostly geologists and volcanologists. They arrived with metal boxes packed with equipment for studying volcanoes. There were lots of reporters and photographers from newspapers, magazines, and television stations. Thousands of sightseers came from all over the country.

Mile-high bursts of steam and ash kept shooting out of the volcano's top, often a dozen times a day. Some of the ash drifted down over the valley. Helen wiped a thin coating of ash off her bicycle almost every morning. It was soft and fine, like gray baby powder.

Helen read in the paper that the governor had declared a 20-mile Red Zone around the mountain's base. The Red Zone was off-limits to everyone but the scientists. Spirit Lake was in the Zone. So were all the summer cabins around the lake, and the Mount St. Helens Lodge. Everyone who lived in the Red Zone was ordered to leave. The owner of the Lodge, Harry Truman, refused to go. Helen had seen Mr. Truman many times when her family was fishing or hiking around Spirit Lake. Helen heard that Harry just laughed at the idea that Mount St. Helens might erupt. The smoke and steam was nothing, he said. It would die down and everything would go back to normal.

But the scientists weren't so sure. Every day they were interviewed by reporters from the newspapers and the television news. Every day they said basically the same thing: there was a lot of activity in and under the mountain. But when the reporters asked them if the mountain was going to erupt tomorrow or the next day, the scientists could only say they didn't know. They tried to explain that it was very difficult to predict what any volcano might do from one moment to the next. But the scientists still cautioned people that Mount St. Helens was potentially very dangerous.

A week passed. Then another and another. Bursts of steam and ash kept spewing from the mountain top at least once a day. But the sightseers who'd been hoping to see a big volcanic eruption began to get impatient.

The scientists kept up their research day and night. Helen often saw them drive past the farm on their way up or down the mountain. The U.S. Geological Survey had two observation stations on Coldwater Ridge. The one called Coldwater II was just six miles from the volcano. From these sites, the scientists kept a close watch on the volcano. They monitored the seismometers on the mountain's slopes around the clock.

Helen went to Rae's Café every afternoon after school. She went on Saturdays, too, always hoping that the scientists might be there grabbing a bite to eat or a quick cup of coffee. On the last Saturday in April, she arrived to find the bearded scientist sitting at a table in the back. He was studying some photographs he'd spread out on the red-and-white checked tablecloth.

Helen grabbed the coffee pot and approached his table shyly. He looked up and smiled. "Hello again, and thank you," he said, holding out his coffee cup for Helen to refill. He noticed her looking at the pictures on the table.

"Would you like to see some pictures of the volcano?" he asked.

Helen's face lit up. "Absolutely!"

The scientist smiled again. "Here, sit down and I will show you something interesting."

Helen glanced around the café. There were only a few other customers at the moment. She could sit for a minute or two. She pulled out a chair and sat down.

"These are pictures we've been taking of the north slope of Mount St. Helens every day for the past few weeks," said the scientist as he laid them out in order on the table. "Notice anything?"

Helen studied the pictures. She spotted the change right away. A big spot on the side of the mountain was growing larger over time. It had started as a raised area. In the most recent photograph, it was a huge bulge.

"That area there," Helen said, pointing at the bulge. "It gets bigger and sticks out farther in each picture."

"You're very observant!" said the scientist. "That bulge has had our attention for some time. We've been using **laser beams** to measure how much the bulge grows every day."

"How can you measure something with laser beams?" Helen asked.

"Well, in simple terms, we bounce them," the scientist said. "From our outposts on Coldwater Ridge we point a laser beam at the mountain. When the beam strikes the mountain, it bounces back. It takes a certain amount of time to do that—a fraction of a second. That time gives us a measurement as to how far away the surface of the mountain is."

Helen understood immediately. "So if the mountain's surface changes, the time it takes for the laser beam to bounce over and back will change, too."

"Exactly!" said the scientist, slapping the table lightly. "And according to our latest laser beam measurements, that bulge is growing at the rate of about five feet per day."

"What's causing the bulge?" Helen asked.

"We think it's the result of magma moving around inside the mountain," he replied.

"Does that mean it's going to erupt sometime soon?" Helen asked quietly.

---

**laser beam** – a narrow, powerful beam of light that can travel across long distances

"Well, that's the big question, isn't it?" he replied thoughtfully. "The frustrating thing about volcanoes is that you never know for sure. That bulge could mean an eruption is on its way. Or it could also stop growing and the whole mountain could calm down."

Helen stared at the pictures of the mountain. She was beginning to realize just how hard it was to predict a volcanic eruption.

 A WEEK AFTER her conversation with the scientist about the bulge on the mountain, Helen was sitting with Chad on the front steps. It was Sunday morning. They were reading the morning paper. Tom was in the kitchen making a fresh pot of coffee.

Chad suddenly looked up from the article he was reading. "Remember when that scientist—David Johnston—compared St. Helens to a dynamite keg?" Chad asked, looking at Helen with a sly grin.

"Yes," Helen replied cautiously.

"Well, that fuse he talked about must be really long."

"What do you mean?" Helen asked.

"Well, it seems that St. Helens is calming down. Just like Dad and I thought it would," he replied. "Here," he said, tossing her the paper. "Read for yourself."

Helen skimmed the first paragraph. Steam and ash had stopped shooting out of the mountain's top. Volcano watchers were leaving. The reporter seemed to think that the long-awaited eruption was not going to happen.

"How can they be sure?" Helen said. "What do the volcanologists say?" She flipped through the rest of the section, hoping to find an article with comments from the scientists.

"Don't know. Don't care," Chad said sarcastically. Then he suddenly leaned closer to Helen. His face was just inches from hers.

"But what I do know, little sister, is that Dave and I are going to be climbing soon," he whispered hoarsely. "And don't you dare tell Dad."

# CHAPTER 5

# More Changes on the Mountain

 THE NEXT DAY after school, Helen hurried over to the café. Rae was busy behind the counter. Helen scanned the room. Her heart sank. None of the scientists were around. But there were quite a few people from Toutle who were sitting together around one table. They were talking loudly. Their voices were angry.

"We've been kept off the mountain for over a month now," a big man proclaimed. "The mountain is calming down. I say it's time we were allowed to go up and check on our property."

"Darn right," agreed a middle-aged woman. "I want to make sure nothing's happened to my cabin at Spirit Lake. I've got my grandmother's china stored up there."

"Well," said a second man, "what are we going to do about it?"

The group lowered their voices. Helen didn't catch any more of their conversation. But two days later, it was obvious what their decision had been. The people at the table, together with other angry property owners, marched out to the roadblock on the highway to Spirit Lake. They staged a protest. They demanded to be allowed into the Red Zone to collect their belongings and check on their cabins. Some threatened to get guns and force their way past the barricade.

Worried that the situation might become violent, the governor agreed to let the protesters travel up to Spirit Lake in a car-and-truck caravan. The date for the caravan was set for Saturday, May 17. Another one was scheduled for the following day at 10 a.m.

The night of the protest, Helen sat on her bed, reading the newspaper. On the editorial page, Helen read an article about the governor's decision and the caravan that was coming up that weekend. She thought the protesters were being rather foolish. Helen wondered what could be so important about old dishes and other stuff that people furnished their cabins with. Going up the mountain to get such things seemed like a silly risk.

Another article caught Helen's eye. It showed a recent photograph of Mount St. Helens. Helen studied it carefully. The bulge was still there. It looked noticeably bigger than it had in the photos that she had seen.

A loud thump from the next room made Helen jump. She slid off her bed and walked down the hall. The door to Chad's room was ajar. Helen tiptoed up and peered into the room. Her brother was crouched over something, tying it shut.

"You OK, Chad?" she asked.

Chad spun around. He stepped backward, trying to block her view of something. But she saw it anyway: his backpack. Beside it was his sleeping bag.

Helen stared at her brother. "What are you doing, Chad?"

"I'm just packing my stuff," Chad snapped. For a split second, he seemed to hesitate. "Dave Ford and I are going fishing this weekend with Dave's uncle," he continued.

"On the Columbia River. Down by Kelso. I already asked Dad. He said it was O.K."

Helen gave her brother a hard, searching look. "Really?" she asked.

"Really," Chad responded. He quickly turned back to what he was doing.

Helen went back to her room and sat down on her bed. During the past year, she and her brother hadn't gotten along very well. They'd fought a lot. But as far as Helen knew, Chad had never lied to her. Yet she had the strangest feeling that that's what he'd just done.

 SATURDAY MORNING, May 17, dawned clear and calm. When Helen got up, she found her father drinking coffee at the kitchen table. "You're up early," she said. "Where's Chad?"

"He's already gone," Tom replied. "Dave picked him up about an hour ago. They've gone fishing on the Columbia River. He said they'll be home sometime late tomorrow afternoon."

"Oh." Helen stood there frowning, not knowing what to think. Part of her doubted that Chad had told the truth about this fishing trip. She opened her mouth to say something to her father. Then she stopped. That little voice had popped into her head again. "Are you sure, Helen? Are you sure Chad is lying?" No, she wasn't sure.

She had no proof that Chad was lying. But the whole thing just felt wrong.

"Come on, kiddo," her father said, seeing her frown. "Eat your breakfast. Then let's go up the road and watch the caravan move out."

An hour later, Tom and Helen were standing by the roadside. Reporters and photographers crowded around the long line of vehicles that stretched behind the barricade. The sheriff was there with some of his deputies. Two National Guard helicopters were there, too—ready in case an emergency evacuation was needed, someone said.

At ten o'clock the deputies pulled the barricade to one side. Cars and pickup trucks slowly passed by as they headed up the mountain. Toward the end of the line, a big red pickup rumbled up. Helen seemed to remember that Jack Ford, Dave's uncle, had a truck like that. The morning sun reflected off the windshield as the pickup rolled past. Helen shut her eyes against the glare. When she opened them, the pickup was past the barricade. Helen watched as the line of vehicles headed slowly up the road and then disappeared behind the first hill.

Late in the afternoon, Helen heard on the radio that the caravan had returned safely. The mountain was quiet. Everything, in fact, appeared to be just fine. But Helen couldn't shake the feeling that something was wrong. The feeling was still there when she went to bed.

# CHAPTER 6

# Eruption!

 HELEN WOKE UP with a start. She sat bolt upright, gasping for breath. She'd had a bad dream. Her brother was standing at the edge of a river, fishing. Then suddenly the water in the river had risen up and washed him away.

Hot and sweaty from the dream, Helen pushed her hair back from her face. Fishing, fishing . . . something about fishing kept tugging at her mind. She looked at the clock: 5:27. It was still dark outside.

She closed her eyes. The dream image of her brother came back again. He was standing there, casting into the water . . .

Helen's eyes flew open. His fishing gear. If he really had gone fishing, he'd have taken it with him. If it wasn't in his room, she would know he had been telling the truth.

Quietly, Helen slipped out of bed and went down the hall to Chad's room. She flicked on the light, squinting against the glare. The door to Chad's closet was shut. Helen opened it and pulled the string that turned on the bare lightbulb overhead. She pushed apart some of the hanging clothes, trying to see into the back of the closet. That's where he kept his fishing rod and tackle box. Helen pawed through a pile of dirty clothes and shoes. No rod and reel. She dug behind a stack of record albums. No tackle box.

Helen stood up and leaned against the closet door. Apparently, Chad had been telling the truth. It was her instincts that had been wrong. Helen sighed. She wanted to feel relieved. But she didn't.

Helen turned out the light in the closet and closed the door. She sat down on Chad's bed. Why did she still feel so uneasy? Chad had left a pile of books on his bed. She reached over to grab the top one. But the book slid out of her fingers and fell to the floor. As Helen bent down to pick it up, she spotted something shiny under the bed. She knelt down and reached into the dusty darkness. Her fingers closed around a small, oval piece of metal. It was a fishing lure—still attached to fishing line! Helen tugged on the line—and Chad's fishing rod slid out from beneath the bed.

With a pounding heart, Helen reached farther under the bed. There was something else there, a hard box with a handle buried beneath what felt like a blanket. She knew it was Chad's tackle box even before she'd pulled it out into the light.

Shaking and dry-mouthed, Helen leaned back against the side of the bed. She thought of the red pickup truck that had been in the caravan that morning. "Chad's up on the mountain," she said to herself. Her brother and Dave Ford were up on Mount St. Helens.

Helen closed her eyes. In her mind's eye, she saw the bulge on the side of the mountain. She remembered what the scientist had said about it—how it was magma moving beneath the surface. She remembered the photograph in the paper—how much the bulge seemed to have grown in just the last few days. And she remembered David Johnston's words: "a keg of dynamite."

Suddenly Helen knew that her brother and his friend were in real danger. She didn't know how she knew it. But she'd never been more sure of anything in her life.

Helen jumped up and sprinted into her father's room. He was snoring lightly. "Dad, wake up!" she cried, grabbing his arm. "Chad's on the mountain and we have to go get him!"

Tom Crenshaw's head jerked up from the pillow.

He squinted at Helen, trying to make sense of what she was saying. "Helen, calm down. Tell me what's going on," he said firmly, sitting up. He flicked on the bedside lamp.

Helen let go of his arm. "Chad's not fishing. He hid his fishing rod and tackle box under his bed. He's up on the mountain, Dad. He wanted to go climbing. I know he and Dave are up there."

"Helen," he said slowly, "how could they have gotten up there?"

"I'm pretty sure they rode up in the back of Mr. Ford's pickup yesterday. In the caravan," Helen replied.

Tom glanced at the clock. "It's only 5:30. The second caravan isn't leaving until ten. We can drive up then and get them."

"No, Dad," Helen replied. Her voice was quiet and calm. "We have to go now."

"Are you sure?" he asked.

"Yes. I'm sure."

There was something in Helen's voice that made Tom pause. He looked at her for what seemed like a long time. "Get dressed," he said suddenly. "Grab your coat and some food and go down to the car."

Five minutes later Tom was pulling out of the driveway and onto the highway. The car sped up the road, headlights slicing through the darkness. About a mile before the barricade, Tom turned sharply off the highway and onto a forest service road. He and almost everyone else in the valley knew a dozen ways up the mountain. He couldn't drive as fast on the narrow service roads. That meant it would take them nearly an hour to reach Spirit Lake. But the way up would be clear.

Tree trunks flashed past. Helen hung on as the car swerved and bumped. "Where do you think they'll be, Dad?" she asked.

"About a mile above the lake, on that little ridge," Tom replied. He gave his daughter a quick smile. "Your brother is a creature of habit, Helen. He always camps there before starting out on a climb."

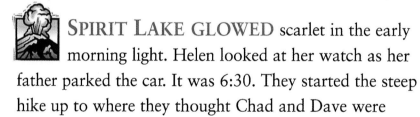 SPIRIT LAKE GLOWED scarlet in the early morning light. Helen looked at her watch as her father parked the car. It was 6:30. They started the steep hike up to where they thought Chad and Dave were probably camped.

Helen stared up at the mountain. It looked quiet, almost peaceful. But the bulge on its north side looked even larger than it had in the photographs.

Forty minutes later, Helen and Tom stepped out into a clearing. Two bright orange tents stood in the shadow of a towering evergreen. Helen heard her father sigh in relief.

"Wake up, boys, it's time to go home," Tom shouted, striding up to the tents. "And Chad Crenshaw, you've got a lot of explaining to do."

Chad came scuttling out of his tent. He stared at his father. Then he turned an angry gaze on Helen. "Dad, I can explain . . . "

Tom cut him off. "Save it, Chad. We'll talk later." Dave emerged from his tent, looking confused. "You and Dave pack up your gear. We're all leaving in 10 minutes."

By eight o'clock they were back at the car. Chad threw his gear into the trunk. Then he grabbed Helen by the arm.

"I know this is your doing, Helen," he hissed. "I won't forget it." Helen pulled away and climbed into the back seat with Dave.

As the car bumped along the furrowed road, no one spoke. The tension in the car seemed thick enough to cut with a knife. Helen kept looking back at the mountain. The sun was shining on it now, lighting up the ash-stained peak. They passed Coldwater Ridge and started down toward the valley. Finally, the familiar glimmer of the Toutle River flashed through the trees.

Helen glanced at her watch. It was 8:30. They would be home in 15 or 20 minutes. She turned to look at the mountain through the back window. Her eyes fixed on the bulge. Suddenly it seemed to move, like a ripple on the surface of a pond.

She blinked her eyes, thinking her eyes were playing tricks on her. Then she realized they weren't.

"DAD!" Helen shrieked from the backseat. "There's something happening on the mountain! LOOK!"

Tom slammed on the brakes. He turned to look where Helen was pointing. As the four of them watched, the entire northern face of Mount St. Helens seemed to ripple and churn. Then it was moving. It was sliding downhill.

Fifteen seconds later, the mountain exploded.

Helen couldn't believe what she was seeing. A jet black plume shot out of the top of the volcano. Then below it, an enormous brown cloud, boiling and churning, erupted from the mountain's north side. It came mushrooming out, getting bigger and bigger by the second. It rolled down the volcano's northern slope, swallowing up everything in its path. It was moving unbelievably fast. And it was coming right at them.

Tom Crenshaw had seen enough. He pressed his foot to the accelerator. The tires spun and the car flew down the dirt track. Helen, Chad, and Dave couldn't tear their eyes away from the erupting volcano. But now that they were moving, they realized the monstrous cloud of ash and hot gases was gaining on them.

"Dad, hurry!" Chad shouted. "It's coming fast!"

Tom glanced in the rearview mirror. He was going as fast as he dared. He knew if he hit a tree they were lost.

The car careened down the road. Now the boiling cloud was so close that Helen could see individual trees disappearing behind them. Above the noise of the car she could hear those trees snapping like matchsticks.

Up ahead the dirt road divided. Tom had to make a split second decision. They had to reach the highway quickly. "Hang on!" he yelled. He jerked the steering wheel hard and the car swerved left. Dave screamed. Helen was too scared to make a sound.

The road ran along a ridge that separated them from the mountain. The cloud was closing in on them. Helen watched in terror as the cloud surged overhead, blocking out the sun. Suddenly they were in a choking hurricane of hot ash. Tom flicked on the headlights. Small rocks fell from the sky like hail, clattering on the roof of the car.

All around them, enormous fir trees whipped back and forth. The ash was getting thicker. It was as black as night now, hot and hard to breathe. Tom could barely see the road.

Helen thought that any second they would die. But the nightmare ride went on and on. Then suddenly the trees opened up. The highway loomed in front of the car. Tom swerved onto the asphalt. He pushed the gas pedal to the floor and the car tore ahead.

After a few minutes, the sky brightened slightly. Less ash was falling here. It was easier to see the road. The huge cloud had roared north from the volcano. Now they were driving almost straight west. They seemed to be moving away from it.

Tom spotted the highway barricade up ahead. He drove off the shoulder and down through the ditch to get around it. When they were back on the highway, Helen looked back toward Mount St. Helens once more. The black plume towered miles above the peak. It was enormous. It seemed to fill most of the sky.

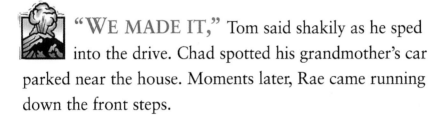 "WE MADE IT," Tom said shakily as he sped into the drive. Chad spotted his grandmother's car parked near the house. Moments later, Rae came running down the front steps.

# CHAPTER 7

# Aftermath

 **8:32 A.M., MAY 18, 1980.** It was a day—a moment—that Helen would never forget. And now Helen was living through another moment she would never forget. Five days had passed since Mount St. Helens had erupted. Helen, Tom, and Chad had spent those days in Toutle, living with Grandma Rae. Now they all stood on a hill above the farm, looking down at what was left of the valley and their home.

The landscape was completely changed. The hills, the road—everything—was covered with thick, powdery, volcanic ash. The river valley was unrecognizable, transformed into a sea of mud, logs, and debris. On the Crenshaw's land, the orchard, pasture, and fields were gone, buried by the mud. Miraculously, the front yard was still there, along with most of the house. What looked like a piece of a bridge had been pushed into the middle of the front porch. But the rest of the house had survived.

Helen had read the newspaper articles written about the eruption over and over again. The scientists had pieced together most of what had happened. When the volcano had exploded, the entire north side of the mountain blew out. Riding on a wave of deadly hot gases, millions of tons of pulverized rock, ash, and chunks of ice from the snow cap went screaming through the air at roughly the speed of sound. Everything within a few miles of the north side of the mountain was wiped out by the blast. When the dust cleared, what was left of the landscape looked like the surface of the moon.

Harry Truman was dead, of course. Mount St. Helens had buried him and the Spirit Lake Lodge under hundreds of feet of ash and stones. David Johnston had been at the Coldwater II station when the eruption started. He'd just had time to radio in one last report: "Vancouver, Vancouver, this is it!" A second later, the young scientist, along with everything else on Coldwater Ridge, was gone. Helen had cried when she heard about his death.

It could have been us, she'd thought at the time. Chad and her father figured that they were alive because of the ridge that lay between the car and the mountain that morning. They'd been protected from the full force of the blast as they were speeding away from the mountain. And they were close enough to the western edge of the blast zone to escape its deadly force.

Helen scanned the hillsides far up the valley. They had once been covered by millions of stately evergreens. But the blast from the eruption flattened all the trees as it tore past. Their branches and bark had been instantly burned away. Only the trunks were left lying on the ground, scattered like straws. On hillsides farther from the mountain, Helen could see some trees still standing. They were all dead, though, killed by the scorching heat.

But the blast had been only the beginning. The intense heat of the eruption had melted most of the snow and ice on the mountain. As billions of gallons of water rushed down the slopes, they mixed with hot ash and pulverized rock. Water and ash combined to form a wall of hot mud that flowed down into the Toutle River Valley.

The mudflow had picked up trees, houses, and barns. It had swept away bridges and miles of road. In parts of the valley, the mud had surged hundreds of feet up the valley walls. It filled the river bend. Many homes along the two forks of the Toutle River had been completely washed away or buried in mud.

Helen's eyes filled with tears as she looked down at what was left of their home—what had been her mother's home, too. But what was important was that she and her family had survived. Including David Johnston and Harry Truman, fifty-seven people had lost their lives during the eruption. Countless numbers of forest animals had died. Helen guessed most of their cattle had been buried by the mudflow. But Jake had shown up just outside of Toutle. He was a little wild-eyed, but otherwise fine.

"We were so lucky," Tom murmured. Helen looked at her father. She grabbed his hand. He gave it a squeeze. Helen turned toward her brother, reaching out with her free hand to catch one of his. But Chad stepped away. He looked at her strangely, and walked off down the hill.

Rae caught the hurt look on Helen's face. "Helen," she said quietly. "Your brother's not mad at you. I think what he's feeling is quite different."

Helen frowned. She didn't know what her grandmother meant. She let go of her father's hand and walked down to where her brother was standing.

"Chad," she said softly. "What's the matter?" Chad hunched his shoulders and said nothing. Helen walked around to face him. "Tell me what's wrong."

At first Helen didn't think her brother had heard her. Then he suddenly reached out and hugged her to his chest. "I'm sorry I lied!" he whispered hoarsely into her ear. "If it hadn't been for you, Dave and I would be dead."

Helen didn't know what to say. She just hugged her brother as hard as she could.

"I think those two are going to be alright," Rae said, turning to Tom.

"She saved his life," Tom responded.

"Yes, for the most part, she did," Rae agreed.

"For the most part?" Tom asked.

"Well, if you hadn't believed in Helen, in her story about Chad being on the mountain, things would have turned out much differently," Rae replied.

Tom was quiet for a moment. "I believed in Helen Sunday morning because she believed in herself," he said. "I heard it in her voice."

Tom looked down the hill at his children. They were crouching now, peering at something in a tangle of grass and ash. Helen looked back and waved. "Come and see what we found!" she cried.

Tom and Rae walked down to meet them. Helen's eyes were sparkling as she held out her hand toward her grandmother. "Well, I'll be," said Rae, when she saw the plump berries in Helen's palm. "Wild salmonberries. Imagine—surviving through all this."

Tom picked up one of the berries and twirled it between his fingers. "Kids," he said quietly. "Do you want to leave the valley? Do you want to leave all this pain and destruction behind?"

Chad sighed, and shook his head. Tom looked at Helen. She felt her stomach tighten. "No, Dad." Then she asked, "Do you?"

Tom looked out over the valley, so utterly different from what it had been just three days before. "No, Helen, I don't. There are a lot of people here who need help now. And we can rebuild the farm." He paused. "I think it's what your mother would have wanted us to do."

Helen felt the knot in her stomach relax. She leaned back against her grandmother and turned her face up to the warm spring sun.

# About Mount St. Helens

▲ Volcanic ash and rock blast from Mount St. Helens.

 BEFORE MAY 18, 1980, Mount St. Helens had been one of the most beautiful and peaceful volcanic peaks in the Cascade Mountain range. At 9,680 feet (2,950 meters), it was the fifth-highest mountain in Washington State.

Most people knew that Mount St. Helens was a dormant volcano. No one was expecting the mountain to erupt.

On March 20, people in towns around the mountain felt an earthquake. This meant that Mount St. Helens had come to life again.

## The Mountain Moves

At the first sign of movement on Mount St. Helens, volcanologists and other scientists rushed to the scene. This was an amazing opportunity. It was a chance to study an awakening volcano firsthand.

The scientists used seismometers to help them monitor the volcano. A seismometer measures movement in Earth's crust. Mount St. Helens was experiencing many small earthquakes. The earthquakes were a sign that melted rock called magma was moving toward the surface.

Scientists were puzzled by a bulge that began to form on the north side of the volcano. The bulge continued to grow until on May 18, a massive earthquake occurred on Mount St. Helens. The earthquake caused the bulge to collapse. Hot gas and steam exploded out from the north side. Huge explosions blasted millions of tons of rock and ash into the air.

## Destruction

The blast from the exploding volcano destroyed the land for several miles. Beyond this blast zone, the trees were flattened.

After the eruption, massive mudflows poured down the side of the volcano. Scientists call these mudflows lahars. Lahars formed on Mount St. Helens when billions of gallons of melted snow and ice mixed with volcanic ash. The hot mud that resulted was as thick as wet cement. It flowed down the mountainsides and into the Toutle River Valley at speeds of up to 50 miles (80 km) per hour.

Thousands of birds, elk, fish, and other animals died during the eruption of Mount St. Helens. Trees were blown down, stripped to bare wood by the heat and scouring action of the blast. Fifty-seven people were killed. However, nearly two hundred people caught in the blast managed to survive. The death toll would have been much higher had the eruption occurred on a weekday, when hundreds of loggers would have been working in the forests.

The effects of the Mount St. Helens eruption were felt beyond Washington State. An enormous column of ash rose 16 miles into the air above the mountaintop. During the first nine hours of the eruption, the volcano coughed out 520 million tons of ash. The fine, powdery ash was carried east by the wind. It spread across eastern Washington, Idaho, and western Montana and into Wyoming. In Spokane, Washington, the ash in the air was so thick that streetlights came on.

## Understanding Volcanoes

Volcanoes form because of the action of magma or hot melted rock. Earth's surface is divided into about 20 huge slabs of rock called tectonic plates. These plates float on a

▼ **The mountain's landscape was covered in miles of dead fir trees.**

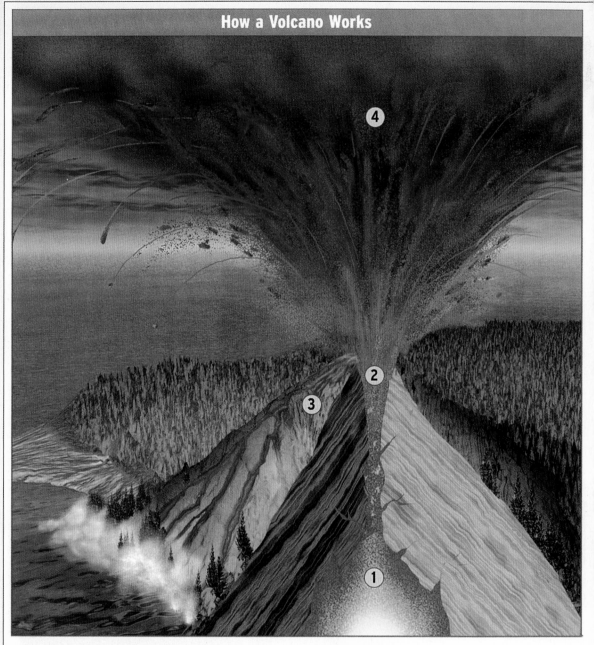

# How a Volcano Works

1. Hot magma from under the surface of Earth creates pressure under the mountain.

2. When too much magma builds up, it moves toward Earth's surface and erupts forming a volcano.

3. As hot lava pours down the sides of the mountain, it cools and hardens. This action builds the volcano.

4. Lava, ash, and rock can blast from a volcano. This material can be seen from miles away.

▲ The blast of the eruption left a huge crater in the mountain.

layer of magma called the mantle. When the plates push against each other, earthquakes occur.

Many of Earth's volcanoes form where two tectonic plates of Earth meet. This area is called a fault.

During an earthquake, these plates can slide past each other horizontally. This is a strike-slip fault. However, if the plates hit each other directly, this can cause the earth to buckle up.

Over time, this buckling action can form mountain ranges, like the Cascades. This action can also force magma to the surface. When magma reaches the surface it is called lava. The lava cools and hardens. Overtime, layers of lava can build up to form a volcano.

## Learning from a Volcano

The eruption of Mount St. Helens was terribly destructive. But it also gave scientists an opportunity. The barren slopes in the blast area and the buried Toutle River Valley became a living laboratory. Scientists came from all over the world to study how nature recovers from a volcanic eruption.

In sheltered spots, some small plants and animals had survived. Plant seeds are carried into the blast zone by the wind and animals. Ants and other insects crawled or flew in. Salmonberries pushed up through nearly a foot of ash. Tiny evergreen tree seedlings took root in what seemed like impossible places—and survived.

Within ten years after the eruption, barren hillsides were covered with small trees and wildflowers. Small animals had returned. After twenty-five years, the trees had grown tall enough to replace much of the forest that had been lost. Herds of elk roam the Toutle River Valley once more. Time and nature have smoothed the rough edges the eruption left behind.

Mount St. Helens has been a model for learning how volcanoes work. After the 1980 eruption, the mountain continued to erupt on a small scale. This gave scientists further opportunities to study an active volcano over a long period of time. They were able to gather vast amounts of data. This data helped scientists understand past volcanic eruptions and predict future eruptions more accurately.

▲ Scientists studied the rocks and minerals that erupted from the volcano.

▲ By 1995, plants and trees had returned to the area around Mount St. Helens.